The Soul Code

The Soul Code

Taylor Moone

IMPRESSUM

TAYLOR MOONE - DER SEELENCODE - First edition

© 2011 Verlag Ingo Simon, St. Wendel
ISBN: 978-3-8391-5363-5

Cover desing: UlinneDesign, Neuenkirchen
Production and publishing: Books on Demand, Norderstedt
ISBN: 978-3-8423-7419-5

Title of the German edition: Der Seelen-Code

German publishing: http://www.verlagis.de
More informationen: http://www.seelencode.com

CONTENTS

INTRODUCTION

The search for meaning is the essence of being human. Fortunately we seek to apprehend or at best understand our own nature, the essence of our soul and the relationship of the earthly and spiritual worlds. In the Western nations, the era of the great religions acting as guardians of the fulfilling thoughts of connection between the world and the creation plan of their Gods, is seemingly coming to an end. To be sure, great faiths are preserved as cultural assets, but the traditional power of definition of its institutions is being increasingly challenged. In recent years, new perspectives and alternative considerations have emerged with increased frequency in the areas of non-religious spirituality. The growing openness of the people to the spiritual side and the knowledgeable individuals - for example, philosophers, theologians, therapists, mediums, or spiritual healers - has transformed the human search for meaning into an common, daily-usage topic. More and more people are trying to find their own, unique purpose in life and live it out. Even if this trend is deplored by representatives of the institutions of great religions, the fact remains that every individual who follows such path finds him or herself closer to his/her soul origin and thus, to the basic creation principle, than many believers that patiently follow the rituals of their religion.

In our earthly interests, we seek quite often material goals and the wealth relating thereto. A major trend in the human search for meaning is its orientation to the visions of an unlimited wish-fulfillment. This cannot be morally reprehensible in any way as it is a deeply human trait and, therefore, understandable. Meanwhile, many books have been written advocating for a modern wishing oracle. Using suitable statements and positive reinforcement, these often proclaim that every human desire will unconditionally come true, provided it does not go in detriment of others.

Rest assured I do not want to appear as opposed to such ideas. Indeed, desires can come true, even if they appear to be eccentric and hardly implementable. A large number of people practice their own personal wishing oracle with great success, following in such case formulation suggestions or rituals of good wishes. It is far from my intent to convince anybody nor do I wish to introduce a better way of wishing. I rather envision my contribution to a full people's life, which I share in my travels and spiritual seminars, to place the meaning of life and thus humanity in the center of the quest for meaning. Thus, my intent is to evidence that there is much more to our lives beyond finding a seemingly effortless way of satisfaction, even if this can be actually quite simple. The central aspect of human life is the soul, held in our body for our entire earthly life. The soul, which comes from the spiritual world and returns there after death, is not poised to find the best path to satisfaction albeit to learn and self-develop. The road to success, whether our search is after philosophical knowledge, material wealth or otherwise, is solely found through the liberation of the deeply set and limitless potential of our soul.

At first sight, this may seem a more demanding endeavor than following a wishing ritual. However, there are two aspects we should remember: Firstly, the development of the soul potential and the creation task of humanity give us the greatest satisfaction on earth, provided we achieve the liberation hence begin to understand the dimensions of our own soul. On the other hand, it is so that the liberation of the soul, as I shall explain in this book, constitutes the operating principle of an ideal oracle through the activation of the soul codes.

Besides all those lucky people who see their wishes come true, stand just as many or even more in utter disappointment, looking for explanations to fathom why their wishes were not fulfilled. At this point, I would like to anticipate the purposes of the book and clarify why so many wishes remain unfulfilled: They do not correlate to the state of the soul.

This does not mean that the souls of those whose wishes have not been heard would be worse or less developed. Nor does it mean that these people would be so punished for something, or excluded from success and happiness. - It just means that the vast potential of your soul is still awaiting the activation of your deeply rooted and indelible soul code. Because this is not active by itself. First, we need to recognize it and then, as you would with a fire, kindle it from a small flame to a burning fire. This is the only reason we are on this planet and thus defines the meaning of life. The unleashing of one's soul potential is the first and foremost task of every individual for his or her own benefit and that of the community of souls. Make your wishes correspond to your soul code status so they become reality as well. For example, the success and recognition we openly desire will arrive if we manage to unleash the potential of our soul and thus to experience the creation principle.

In this book, I intend to describe the soul code for you while providing an opportunity to perceive how active your soul code is already. As you understand that the soul code we all carry within us and the creation principle are one and the same thing, your soul will further develop and the effect of the code will grow. You will realize that it suffices to set it in motion once and then let go to lead a fulfilling live and turn wishes into reality.

Furthermore, I will tell you about Joshua - a soul seeking for the meaning of life as we all do. Joshua will help you delve deeper and understand the soul code.

The basis of this book is a lecture that I have held in numerous seminars before meaning-seeking people. Indeed, it was them who allowed me to create the lecture contents thus making the connections of the soul code available to as many people as possible. I would consider the purpose of this book fulfilled if I contributed to my readers' search for meaning.

PART I

RECOGNIZING THE SOUL

THE SELF-DEVELOPMENT PRINCIPLE

Anthropology has always pondered over the human nature question. From the perspective of anthropological optimism, men are a blank slate at birth, developing their character and traits only in contact with their material and social environment. Conversely, the pessimistic position assumes that the whole essence of a person is genetically determined and thus can hardly be influenced by education or other social contacts. However, this fundamental dispute stems from neither anthropology nor other sciences. It is fed by religious fundamentalisms found in various cultures, hence is as old as humanity itself.

In Western societies, it is primarily teachers and psychologists who deal with the human nature question. The reality of human interaction persists regardless of the fact that people adapt, changing sometimes even permanently. At a minimum, the sanction systems of human societies reflect the simple basic formula of cause and effect. Misconduct is sanctioned according to a written and limit-constrained action plan - with the aim to suppress the unwanted behavior and reward the socially desirable and thus adapted or welfare-promoting one. At the same time, familiar and socially ordered educators are working to build the proper behavior using their own insight and the value of constructive co-existence.

The educational, psychological and religious realism have been introduced with certain delay in Human sciences. We have reached a compromise between the formerly entrenched fronts: This means that probably some of what constitutes the human nature and the individual development is innate or is at least defined or limited in its ability to develop, and that other adaptability areas are subject to social relations and actions. The suspicion remains that the traditional, centuries-old scientific theory has come to a conclusion that could have been drawn before on any daily endeavor. There seems to be a "red thread" of the spiritual science that, after a long dispute, captures what humanity knew intuitively all along.

Unfortunately, the soul is hardly the subject of scientific observation. In most cases, only religions consider the laws of the soul. However, the soul is usually understood as the indelible instance that transcends the material world after death and that, in its non-tangible form, travels to a world beyond for a limited time or to never return. As seemingly abstract and above all theoretical construct, the soul remains devoid of any scientific consideration. On the positive side, we should point out that this does not prevent millions of people to start from the existence of the human soul to design a picture of their nature and functions in connection with religion or personal faith.

Psychology and Psychiatry provide further confusion when they speak of "mental disorders" or "mental illness" and thus describe mental states. Psyche and soul are therefore often used as synonymous terms. Of course, this approach is justified in a society that claims religious freedom for itself. From a personal standpoint, I am against this oversimplification of terms. To clarify from the start to the readers of the book my basic attitude towards the human soul, which springs from my spiritual experience, I would like to stress the following: In my experience, the soul is one's own instance and not identical or even similar to what we refer to as psyche. Body and psyche of the people belong to their earthly existence of the material world in which we live. The soul, which outlasts the life of the world, is the only independent instance of this matter.

Our earthly life is available in all its fullness and all its forms to understand the essence and functions of the soul. Furthermore, the other-worldly -the spiritual- world lies open for us with all its love. This we achieve in different ways, receiving information and messages that tell us about and draw us closer to our own nature. I am often asked why the door to the spiritual world is not open to everyone but only to certain randomly selected individuals, or to those endowed with particular talents. My answer is a simple message: The spiritual world is open to everyone. This is where we come from and where we shall return. In a certain way, we live constantly in it and are always surrounded by it. The most demanding and complex learning task of the soul is to recognize and reactivate the connection between earthly existence and the spiritual world. Those up to this task live a full life on earth and are simultaneously aware of the spiritual world. If this consciousness or awareness of the spiritual world is concurrent to all earthly existence, provided this is not lip-service or imagined but a truly experienced one, then the spiritual world would be as open to us as the earthly one is. People who have reached this stage of development see dead souls and angels and are able to heal without training.

These abilities, present in all of us, may not be uncovered by each living man up to his death. That is not how human life is created. It takes more than an earthly life in order to achieve this soul development state. Nevertheless, many people today can attain this state as they have frequently experienced it and further developed their souls. Hopefully, I will be able to provide all interested souls who read this book with a little help on their way. Upon reading this book, such souls will be intuitively reminded of their own nature and continue on their way. I write with a desire to help the spiritual development of multiple souls while paving a path to their natural destination. Admittedly, much of our earthly existence is already established and the possibilities or influence opportunities are sometimes limited. However, provided we follow our own best-determination, the development and advancement of the soul lies largely in our hands.

We are born with this ability, this urge for soul development. Our soul is not subject to the confines of earthly matter. From a human standpoint, it appears infinite and limitless. In our earthly life, the soul is constrained in the corset of the human organism to learn how to self-develop. It stores all information of our experiences, thoughts, and feelings. The soul matures through experience that it captures after death in the form of the earthly existence and carries forward as assets or talents to the next life on earth. Accordingly, in our lives we are bound to accept challenges, overcome obstacles, set goals and work towards their achievement.

However, this does not mean that we become smarter or more successful with each rebirth. The existence form of our organism is neither a mirror of the soul development nor a reward of sorts for fulfilling learning tasks. Thus, a highly evolved soul may be born with a severe intellectual disability or in a totally amoral milieu. Conversely, a young and hence barely educated soul may attain a very high level of education or live surrounded by wealth and prosperity. Let us suppose that a very advanced soul was assigned the primary learning task of further developing charity and generosity on earth. - In a life characterized by wealth and material security, this learning task may not pose a particular challenge. However, the same challenge living in poverty would represent a much serious endeavor. From the soul perspective, living in poverty may prove a much more interesting and instructive experience. Conversely, however, it should not be inferred from this example that experienced souls are exposed to increasingly adverse conditions with each new life. There are multiple and varied reasons why a soul may be born into a particular life on earth. In the second part of the book, I will talk about the karma that answers such question.

Human learning tasks appear on the demands of everyday life and in the talents and skills of a newborn. Above all, it is about the use of individual talents. It is not about personal success, wealth or other benefits that could be achieved with the development of talent. These are basically side-effects, which are to some extent appropriate and justified. Everyone has the blessing of the universe, if he lives commensurately with the fruits of his deeds or decisions. This is neither the compensation nor the curse of a talent, but simply the mundane running of a successful talent development. The spiritual world measures the value of a soul development mainly through the amount of love the corresponding human soul brings into the world in its human existence using the provided and later developed talents and abilities. Simply put, it is about how much good we have done to others by using our skills. Needless to say, it goes far beyond the great talents of poets, thinkers, artists, athletes, scholars, and philosophers. It is about talents that we carry along in every moment of our lives. Using our talents, we can do some good every day.

The theories of evolution are based on the selfish attitude of all earthly beings. After the principle of the conservation of species was disused by science, a new concept was needed which could explain the progress of evolution the same way as the social behavior of humans and animals. Behavioral research has attempted to explain actual unselfish behavior to extreme altruism using selfish intents. Stated in a simple and certainly shortened formula, it assumes that everything that a living being does is driven by the purposes of selfish self-preservation and the selfish passing of one's own gene pool. Therefore, it must be assumed that every person is born as an egoist who adopts a social behavior whenever a benefit may ensue or the pass-on of its gene pool is assured. Certainly, this theory has its scientific and possibly pragmatic advantages. I do not wish to discuss the results of ethnology at this point. I like to take them as earthly truth, unless a more sustainable explanation model is provided. In my view, it seems especially important to explain at this point that these theories will not describe the nature of the human soul. Human endeavor, including the operation and rules of the human psyche, are certainly very comprehensible and simple to describe. Along those lines, it may be possible that the egoistic explanation provides important predictions on human behavior.

However, it does not describe the basic principle of the human soul. I have already explained that soul and psyche are two different instances of human existence. Hence, we come upon the question of the role the human soul plays in human selfishness. Let us first consider how this human selfishness is exactly displayed. To that end, I would like to direct our attention to the birth of the human condition instead of discussing various examples. Already at birth, and especially during the first period thereafter where life experiences are still very limited, the supposed selfishness and the essence of the human soul should appear together. So, is there such selfishness in the soul? How is the soul related to this phenomenon?

The soul in the spiritual world is not bound by the same limits of earthly existence. In reality, our human organism is a really small housing for an originally large and free soul. After death - or more precisely, between two earthly lives - our soul is not bound as individuals are. The soul would not seek such a state there anyway. It is part of a whole. In other words, it is deeply connected with the other souls while melting into the totality of the divine beauty and harmony. Such state is inconceivable in this world. The active part of our soul in earthly life has no memory thereof hence cannot develop such feeling. Presumably, the soul would not want to dwell on this earth should it feel what existence form awaits after death. At the same time, however, it displays a profound intuition and a deep-seated longing for the harmony. Our soul seeks to escape the confines of our bodies and our earthly mind, this simple human psyche. It aims to spread and connect with the divine harmony and unity of the spiritual world.

Measured against the possibilities of the soul before birth, it feels uncomfortable and constrained in an earthly body. The soul seeks harmony and balance in order to develop at will. From this desire for higher development emerges the human urge for need satisfaction, warmth, affection, and protection. From an earthly perspective, the attempts of a new baby to create a pleasant state of his own at any cost may be perceived as selfish behavior. However, why does a baby behave in such a way? Is it possibly an instinctive survival mechanism at play? Maybe it is because it lacks any social behavior? - I believe the answer is simpler and at the same time, more original: In doing so, the soul is desperately trying to restore the state of its origin. The human selfishness is not limitless. There could be no welfare state societies should strict egoism form the essence of human nature. The human primal horde would not have survived - at least not as sense-seeking and culture-creating beings. Division of labor and power as well as consideration and therefore, to some extent the social behavior could possibly be attributed to the conventions of an animal herd. Religion and art as well as their associated traditions would not have emerged as essential cornerstones of any culture.

Hence, there is more than selfish instinct to the newborn. Admittedly, a very self-centered behavior emerges from his vulnerability and helplessness on the one hand, and from his lack of experience and maturation on the other hand. This, however, cannot be regarded as a fundamental human trait. The human soul longs for its origin and is striving to return to the spiritual world. The memory of those deprived directs the human activity towards the creation of the kingdom of heaven on earth. That does not necessarily produce good deeds but regularly leads to conflict and disappointment. Oftentimes, the human soul seeks the optimal conditions in the distress of its earthly limitations.

THE PATH OF HUMANITY

The task of every human being is the constructive development of his own soul, which seeks to disentangle itself from the human body it is trapped in. As simple as it may sound, we do have basically only one purpose in life - to fulfill its needs, hard or unfeasible as it might be at times, inasmuch as we can. The physical constraints of earthly existence and the temptations of the material world can easily distract us from the search for meaning and thus also of the liberation of our soul.

However, the actual objective pursued cannot be reached in such a way. Individuals are able to gain knowledge and enlightenment so that they better understand God's plan as well as the nature and destiny of the human soul. The completion of creation, that is heaven on earth, can be reached only in the coexistence of souls. This collective learning task of the souls is little known and its implementation in this world still lies in the distant future.

In the spiritual world, we usually refer to as "Beyond" from our earthly point of view, the whole as a union of souls is as evident as the individuality of the individual is on earth. A contribution to the community of souls seeking the development of the whole rather than the individual one is neither dangerous nor difficult in the spiritual world. Nevertheless, deceased souls can deny themselves the wisdom and love of the spiritual world. In both forms of existence, it is our obligation to allow the community to benefit from our soul development state. The purpose of creation is fulfilled when humanity has evolved to the point that earthly existence correlates with the spiritual world. Both forms of existence are then merged together. While humanity is certainly far from this point today, I am utterly convinced that we will follow this path to its end: the path of soul liberation!

THE HIDDEN CODE

While our task is to harness the full potential of our soul through constant development and to achieve thereby an increasingly higher form of existence, there is also a useful principle for us to fulfill such task. Deep inside us - in an area that we possibly refer to "the unconscious" in our earthly understanding - we have an intuitive and visionary idea of the possibilities of our soul. The engine that drives our search for meaning is firmly rooted in us, even if we may not have immediately retrievable understanding of the development goals of the soul, that is, the attainment of a higher state of development of one's soul and the further development of the community of souls.

But how does our soul operate? What are the principles upon which it can be developed? How is it able to achieve a higher level? What is the creation principle underlying it? Can we decipher the code of the soul itself?

The answer is easy: Yes, we can do so because it is shown to us every day. For our entire earthly existence, life reveals to us the soul code. The real challenge does not lie in recognizing or understanding it. It is rather about allowing itself to become self-conscious and aware and thus develop and truly experience the creation principle.

The overall soul code can be broken down in four areas, which can be specifically used and addressed. I shall describe these four areas as four individual soul codes. From the code *of love, the code of community,* the *code of resonance,* and the *code of karma* emerges much more than just the operating principle of the soul. Indeed, from them arise the creation principle and the soul code, for both are basically one and the same. The soul code lies deep within us, like a hidden treasure worth being recovered. It is like a book of knowledge that is waiting to be opened and read. Open the book of your soul and read it!

PART II

THE FOUR SOUL CODES

1

THE SOUL CODE OF LOVE

The spiritual world is flooded with infinite love. The full and unlimited access to the community of souls is waiting there for us and will be given to us after death as a divine gift. Our soul carries along the deep knowledge of this fact and makes us seek such fulfillment for our entire life. A large variety of human endeavors are necessary to achieve the security of the boundless love. We have already seen that seemingly egoistic traits and characters excel and then desperately seek a spurious earthly fulfillment. Behind it stands the quest for something higher, the yearning for the transcendent bond. Recognizing this and becoming aware of such destiny belongs to our spiritual learning tasks. We carry a deep longing for affection in our worldly existence. From birth, we strive to receive unconditional affection as the earthly form of Love. Children born into favorable circumstances receive the unconditional affection of their mother. After our soul has apparently lost the unlimited community and the permanent connection to the other souls in the process of incarnation, we feel a piece of heaven in the maternal affection of the first few days.

However, the baby soon realizes that earthly affection is limited - it is not even unconditional. Day after day, new demands are placed on interpersonal affection. One of the first experiences of conditional sympathy lies in the fact that the simple screams of the baby may lead to the denial of the affection desired and initially received without reservations. Relaxed parents provide more warmth and affection upon the unnerving night cry of the baby pleading for unconditional affection. Parents who have experienced little love often tend to withhold love. Life experiences, individual life stories and in no minor measure, personality traits influence our ability and willingness to give love. This impacts not just the affection for the child, but the ability to love in any sort of relationship. Unconditional love, especially for the purposes of charity towards strangers, is a very ambitious goal, equivalent to the attainment of the highest possible level of earthly evolution. Given that we seek absolute love as individuals, two or more people meeting for the first time display identical emotional intentions. Initially, it looks pretty simple: Both partners could give each other their unconditional affection. Both pursue the same goal and should therefore be able to agree on their practices. Now, why does this seldom work?

It is in the earthly nature that unconditional affection can only be given by one person? If so, attempting to do so with an additional partner will see the first one renouncing to part of this love, at least temporarily. We were already forced to find a rule or a procedure that manages the distribution of our affection. There is no solution to this dilemma in a physical world. For love is usually considered quite substantive -as objective as a reservoir that would be distributed. On closer inspection, such love is a feeling that could be equally directed at two people. Hence, we expect certain actions as a result of this feeling as the need for sharing appears. However, even here we find an observation error: Love is neither external nor an internal sense of affection.

Love is a state. Such state is free of judgments and intentions. We find ourselves in a conscious awareness of our feelings and our thoughts, free from our own or anybody else's evaluation. We do not act and we do not plan, we simply *are*. In this state, we can accept and forgive. We do not strive for material wealth or external conveniences. We consciously perceive what is happening around us and are filled with positive thoughts. This existence, which we refer to as otherworldly from our earthly standpoint, is evident to a soul in the spiritual world. In our worldly existence, it seems to be an almost unattainable goal.

However, after this state our longing to return reappears. Limited to the physical world, we develop a quest for external affection. The daily life shows us, however, that this affection is neither unconditionally received nor given. And all of our frustrations in dealing with the earthly love make us more and more tempted to seek the external affection - even if we crack upon it. Hence, we seldom seek the love *state*, even though it constitutes the deep desire of our soul.

> ### Soul code 1
> *The human soul seeks the unconditional love state to live it together with others.*

This dream, this sense-seeking quest is what keeps us alive and lets us proceed with our earthly search for meaning. It constitutes the only driver for our desire for knowledge and our spirit of search in a seemingly often nonsensical world. In addition, we seek this knowledge externally. However, the true meaning of life lies in us. The self-discovery and further development of the soul is the sole and all-fulfilling sense of earthly life. Therefore, we return back to earth over and over again. We do so to attain an additional maturity for our soul and understand it better.

There are religious approaches that arise from an universal, immutable soul. It becomes thus an inviolable instance that requires no further development. To be sure, a sense of earthly life may also be derived from such religious approaches. However, I am deeply convinced that despite of its size and openness, its skills and talents, and the worldly existence, the soul will be born simply in a field of unconditional love, developing and prospering over time. Time is a difficult concept to grasp, because it does not exist as such in the spiritual world. This phenomenon is an earthly concoction designed to make processes livable and describable. Our limited understanding seems to help the acceptance of time in the understanding of our world. Hence, I use the term as well. Since the soul will be born again in human form to learn on Earth, its development seems to take in our view a very long time, maybe even a never-ending one.

Joshua and the Angel of Earth - Part 1

Joshua called upon the earth angel to fathom the human essence. He asked the angel for help with his suggestion, because he could not obtain the human essence from the spiritual world in which he lived. Since he had never lived on earth, this journey of souls drew his interest, and he wanted nothing more than the first birth on earth.

"Angel of Earth, how should a human be? Please explain to me this existence and help me understand."

The angel required Joshua to enumerate his learning tasks and to describe how far he had progressed in his knowledge.

"I pursued the learning task of unconditional love." Joshua said, and did not understand what the point of the angel's question was.

"What do you know about the unconditional love and to what extent can experience it, Joshua?"

"I do not know", Joshua said. "Unconditional love is the experienced togetherness of two or more souls, without mutual claims. I have read so in the book of my life and how it applied to me. Still, I do not understand it. How could conditioned souls give love? Why should I expect any compensation for giving my love? Furthermore, what could a soul provide I did not already have?"

The Angel of Earth smiled and said: "Now, what would happen if you were alone? If no other souls kept your company, to give you their love to you while receiving yours? What would happen if I were not here, and there was only you? What would you do, Joshua?"

Joshua considered the question. However, he failed to envision the situation. Indeed, he had never been alone. The answer came to him only with difficulty, as he was continuously connected to other souls and endowed with divine wisdom.

"I reckon", he began hesitantly, "I would try to return here and remain connected to all, as it is now."

The Angel of Earth knew that soon the time would come to send Joshua's soul to Earth so that he may find the answer to his question.

"My dear Joshua, do you think then that you could wish nothing but to seek love if you lost it? Moreover, should you be separated from other souls, do you believe you would immediately spread love to be reunited with the others?"

"Yes, I probably would. Yes, I'm sure of it. Angels of Earth, have I understood Love?"

"I am afraid not, Joshua. You have not understood it. You had it as gift hitherto. You're surrounded by it and it was given to you unconditionally. You will understand its value quickly."

As the time came for Joshua to visit Earth for the first time, the Angel of Earth called him again.

"Joshua, your time has come. Today, I am sending you to Earth. Your first life on Earth is waiting for you. In the first years of your earthly existence, you will gradually forget me only to remember me again after your death. I *will offer you multiple opportunities to experience unconditional love so you can learn your lesson."*

And so, Joshua was born. He fell asleep and woke up as a baby in the arms of his earthly mother. He was startled because he was incredibly close to his body. His own soul was the only one he could perceive. He felt lonely, abandoned, and separated from what had been familiar and reliable. Cold and fear conquered his body and his mind. An unknown inner pain invaded him. He was overpowered by the feeling of being lost and of the once ubiquitous, now wrested from him love.

"Angel of Earth," he said anxiously, "What have you done to me? Why did you send me in this terrible world? "

Separated from the infinite and unconditional love, Joshua longed in the very first moment of his earthly life to return and experience love once again. Joshua tried to let heaven know about his feeling of abandonment and separation, the desire for love and affection, and his longing to connect with the divine wisdom and all the other souls. However, as he had no language yet in his earthly life, he joined instead

The earthly form of love between two people, for example, between mother and child or between two friends or lovers, constitutes a training ground for the soul. It learns about the form of conditional love. After earthly death, the particular experience in this field is used to join the community of souls. Because this does not happen automatically. We die with all the thoughts, attitudes, and the consideration of love and charity we favored during our lifetime on earth. Moreover, we are not automatically transferred to our former soul state. As earthbound spirits, we may become trapped by the earthly reality and thus remain between two worlds as earthly human spirits. Such earthbound spirits, unable to let go and move into the light and thus into the world of souls, are frequently unaware that they are already dead. Mediums in contacts with the world of the deceased provide different reports and information on why these unconscious spirits remain stuck in the earthly world. My belief is simple: It is the failure of such souls to embrace true love that holds them here. In the state of love, no soul does depend on earthly things after death. It would enter joyfully into the communion of souls.

Activation of the Soul Code of Love

The first soul code, the code of love, is free and bubbles up as an inexhaustible source, whenever we experience the following sentiments:

1. **We no longer wish to change people.**

   We let them be who they are. We experience and acknowledge their beliefs, attitudes, and all their feelings and thoughts, because we recognize the diversity of creation in them. It does not matter whether we find such attitudes and thoughts in ourselves or whether we agree with them.

2. **We avoid judging what or how someone is.**

   It is important not to judge what a person is. If we allow others to be themselves, it is also possible to suspend any judgmental assessment and entertain positive thoughts instead.

3. *We rejoice in the success of others.*

We grant other people's success whole-heartedly. Envy and jealousy are alien to us. We avoid assessing whether it is them or us who deserves success the most. We look forward to hearing from other people's successes - even with successes as earthly as economic prosperity or public notoriety.

However, favoring a non-judgmental stance and letting others be themselves is not always an easy task. This is specially so because we tend to judge behavior. Doing this is correct. We cannot live in a chaotic, unregulated environment and, therefore, we rely permanently on a behavior rating system and derive consequences from it. We are on the right track when we understand that our assessment may relate to behavior and at the same time, suspend our verdict on the person's nature.

The soul code is activated mainly through knowledge. We are aware and accept it so we keep him in custody as it begins to unfold. For each code, I propose a simple exercise that can help you better identify and activate each code. Upon a first reading of the book, you may realize that your soul code is not as active as you thought. On the preceding pages, I have presented a brief overview of how an active code of love can be recognized. Please provide an honest estimate of your agreement level with each specific item. Do you experience such feelings frequently or, conversely, you find it difficult to accept this position?

Do not worry if it proves difficult to complete. By performing simple exercises, you can liberate or further foster the initial as well as additional codes.

Exercise for the soul code of love

Take some notes by hand and write on each one the name of a successful person you may not know or maybe even dislike. Choose either known members of the public or the media or those who you know from your own circle of acquaintances. Your reference to these people may be connected to their financial success or positions of power, or something else that you deem as a great success. Now take each piece of paper in the hand and present the person exactly. Then say:

"I do not begrudge this success. Some good can come of it. "

Put the piece of paper to the side and then take the next one. Repeat the process. Repeat this exercise in the next few days until you can say the sentence confidently, with a positive feeling.

2

THE SOUL CODE OF COMMUNITY

Man is born as a social being. He cannot help but to turn to other people and seek their vicinity. The spirit progressively atrophies if denied contact with other people. If we consider that the soul in the spiritual world is not familiar with the state of solitude, we can easily understand that the earthly existence of the men's soul is filled with the desire for unity with others. Hence, our fellow human beings perform an important function. For they are the ones who can give us some tender loving care. Even the newborns seek this form of contact. Throughout our lives, we never stop seeking positive attention. Even desperate, disappointed in social contact or tortured people, cherish the desire for agreeable affection, for the warmth and love we give one another. However, the togetherness of the people cannot work to everyone's content if each one of them seeks as much affection as possible. Who should provide this without partially separating from his own claim to the attention of others? Since love is generally perceived and envisioned as a beneficial action, this desire remains often unfulfilled. Appreciating devotion and attention, affectionate physical contact and emotional or material support in difficult situations, is likely to be interpreted by many as a sign of love or charity. The denial of these attentions results from the withdrawal or lack of love. The human need to receive this positive attention as intense and often as possible, is so strong that we often deny ourselves just to obtain it: We adapt and adjust ourselves to please the people whose earthly love we seek. Even children learn to behave in a certain ways to experience positive attention. This is probably inevitable in the educational process. Unfortunately, we learn as children that certain feelings are not desirable, that we should not allow ourselves to feel anger or sadness in given situations. We suppress these unpleasant feelings and adjust accordingly to obtain such positive attention. Over time, this inevitably leads to a partial loss of the feeling for our actual emotions. At some point, we need to stop repressing these unwanted emotional states. We fail to feel them and wrongly assume to be feeling something else.

If we have learned that anger is an appropriate emotion in situations that make us really upset, we feel the anger only and forget that we are really playing such emotion. We can no longer distinguish between our true feelings and our self-expression. Over the course of our life, we develop a self-concept that represents a compromise between our deepest feelings and the expectations of our fellow human beings. However, it would be better for us if we were always aware of our true feelings. We could be more authentic or at least let our thoughts be so. Truth to be told, it is not possible to behave ourselves permanently according to our true feelings - even if we could always take it and wanted to act accordingly. The freedom of action on earth can never be infinite, because it would violate and possibly destroy numerous rights and freedoms of others. That cannot really be the goal of human development. Conversely, it can and must be the intent to rediscover the true feelings and allow their expression.

Accordingly, we must find opportunities to express our feelings and remain continuously aware of their existence. This would happen without conflict should we find fellow humans who lend themselves to hear our feelings and let them be that way.

We are experiencing two fundamental difficulties in social contact with other people. The first difficulty arises from our search for a full cooperation because of the original nature of our soul. In our earthly housing, we are looking for positive affection, warmth, and protection by doing so. Simply put, we are looking for the love of others. We frequently adjust our lives to that end. The second difficulty is that we are challenged by others as love-giving people. Even our fellow human beings seek fulfillment through affection. Accordingly, we will even provide the "offenders", which demand certain feelings and attitudes, certain relief out of our sympathy.

> ### *Soul code 2*
> *The human soul seeks an honest and sincere connection to others.*

It belongs to our earthly task to uncover a common path with our fellow human beings that drives a solid commitment. Love cannot be lived on a give and take basis. The earthly form of affection will never be unconditional. Therefore, it is key to achieve the original form of love. Such love is inherent to the soul. Such love has no feeling and no action. It neither demands nor requires. It neither plans nor acts. Love *is*. Understanding this is possibly one of the greatest challenges of human existence.

Frequently, contacts between the two people leave one of the parties feeling better afterwards and the other worn out and tired. The loss of strength may be the result of a compassionate response: On the assumption that our companion is suffering, we assume a similar stance and deplore his fate with him. So no one finds help. This form of companionship suppresses their code of community. Conversely, if we manage to feel compassion, we accompany these people in a caring and pleasant way albeit keeping our feelings to ourselves. We do not feel worn out and ponder thoughtfully on the situation although with our own feeling. Our fellow human beings will benefit from it and experience our honest companionship. In doing so, the soul code of community is activated or further developed. Certainly, it is difficult to simultaneously protect ourselves against energy loss and experience feelings of compassion in contact with people. However, this task also belongs to humanity. The easiest way out of the risk of compassion or the feeling of being exploited emotionally would be the personal isolation. While retired and solitary living minimizes the risk of losing oneself in contact with others, it does so at the hefty price of earthly loneliness and shutdown of our soul development. However, this does not mean that multiple interpersonal relations or even enduring long-term, painful relationships would be necessary to develop the code of community and to fulfill the tasks associated thereto. In fact, is the quality of our relationship building that makes a difference. The decisive factors are the intensity and dedication whereby we build the relationships with other people, but also our thoughts and feelings towards them. Thousand well-meaning encounters with other people deemed as good-natured, generous and helpful in an earthly sense may yield no appreciable benefit if our help or assistance is driven by our selfish goals, or our actions are not impelled by compassion or charity. However, a single, momentary encounter between two people, even for a fleeing instant, could wake up and foster the code of community or further rekindle the long flickering fire of the soul. To that end, such brief moment should be free from demands or interests that people impose on each other, while being influenced by the realization that our contrary is part of the soul community and will always remain so.

If we can say with conviction what we see in other people: *That too is a part of me,* even or especially upon other's rejection, we have fathomed the code of community. We experience it in its highest possible earthly form. This does not mean, however, that we would be inclined to agree with the decisions or actions of other people at all times. Charity, tolerance, acceptance and a non-judgmental compassion does not mean granting every person the randomness of his earthly actions. As humans, we are frequently fraught with uncertainty and doubt, issue judgments on other's behaviors, and derive consequences thereof. Above all, understanding that our fellow human beings are part of ourselves and thus part of the community of souls, means accepting without judgment their inner nature and therefore their soul as part of the whole.

Joshua and the Angel of Earth - Part 2

Joshua came upon the Angel of Earth to describe his early life. In particular, he depicted all his experiences, feelings and sensations - everything he experienced on earth for the first time. He covered many interesting encounters and events albeit some experiences of suffering and worry as well. Among other things, he endured the painful experience of losing a good friend whose deception blemished the trust he initially earned.

"Tell me, Angel of Earth, have I fulfilled my duties?" Joshua asked.

"Joshua, it is not about whether you have fulfilled your duties but how did you deal with them. As you know, life on Earth is about developing your soul to learn and thus to contribute to the progress of the community of souls. You cannot learn everything at once. However, everything you have already fathomed and implemented in this life will be given to you as strength of character in your next one - as the foundation of your personality. Certain elements you have already learned will be presented as new when you are re-born, as you have not yet accepted the inherent task."

"What task was that?" Joshua said.

"As your trusted friend deceived and betrayed you, you were offered the challenge to recognize the community of souls. However, moved by your pain and desire for retribution, you chose to fill yourself with hatred and banish your former friend. You stopped seeing him as part of the community", the Angel of Earth said.

Joshua though it over, remembering the anger and frustration that overtook him after breaking up with his trusted friend.

"What did you expect from me instead? Should I have forgiven that friend? Should I have tried to amend our tarnished friendship? "Joshua asked, desperately.

"Joshua", replied the Angel of Earth, "you know that no one holds any expectations on your behavior. Such disagreement was written in the book of your life from the very beginning of your friendship. The following pages were empty though. Whatever you decision was, whether to further pursue that friendship of abandon it, should not have led you to forget the community of souls. Carried away by anger, you desired your friend's life end. In fact, you excluded him from the community of souls."

"Yes, I did. The friend's betrayal was so painful that I deemed his happiness wholly undeserved."

"Joshua, once your anger had somewhat abated, you spoke of him only as a traitor and no longer a friend. In hindsight, you concluded that your friendship was never worth anything. May I ask you now, whether you believe this assessment still holds true? Before you answer though, please recall whether your time together before the betrayal was just a worthless period full of deception, in which your supposed friend did you wrong secretly. If so, then your assessment would apply, and your task of making a contribution to your soul community out of such conflict, shall be deemed as fulfilled. However, this would not be so if you can certainly state that your friendship was once honest and sincere, and that your rage denied this truth its due acknowledgment. In view of this, what should your answer be, Joshua? "

Joshua looked down. He began to understand and see what he was not willing to see in his lifetime.

"Angel of Earth, I was wrong. Our friendship was once the most precious asset in my life. It meant more to me than any other relation-

ship. That explains why my friend's betrayal was such a painful experience. Nevertheless, I cannot say that the perceived honesty and sincerity of our friendship before this event would have been a fake or preposterous one. No, it was an honest friendship until that day. I can feel that precisely now. "

"Do you still want to know what was expected of you, Joshua?" the Angel of Earth said.

"I know it already," Joshua said. "I could have turned away from my friend while keeping all the good we had as a precious remembrance. I could have condemned the act itself while leaving my friend's essence untouched by my judgment. Had my angry wishes been fulfilled, I would have excluded his soul from the communion of souls. In doing so, I would have separated my soul from the community as well. In this part of myself, I have become blocked and sealed, stopping my own development."

Joshua felt sad because he deeply regretted having done so much against his own nature and destiny. However, it was failing to recognize this that he regarded as utterly incomprehensible. He began to weep, overpowered and ashamed by his own humanity and fallibility in the earthly existence.

In our human understanding, it sometimes proves difficult to distinguish between the being and the actions of a person. At first glance, it may seem plausible or even correct to assume that a man acts the way he thinks and vice versa. Accordingly, a simple formula could be: Whoever does evil thinks evil and thus must be evil. As we question ourselves critically, there is no denying we frequently entertain thoughts or fantasies we will never implement because of our moral understanding or ethical or religious education. At times, these are violent fantasies of revenge on an individual who has supposedly done us some wrong. Alternatively, we wish him to suffer exactly as we did or endure a fatal turn of fate that would take away something valuable or beloved. There are multiple thoughts of revenge and also those unrelated to retribution yet including the notion of harm to others. In any case, the fact that we entertain such thoughts does not lead to consider ourselves evil or mean persons. However, this has less to do with the fact that we regard our fantasies as due compensation for the experience of suffering. It is mainly because we are positive such fantasies will never be implemented.

It may be true that wrong or immoral actions can only be born out of vicious thoughts. Nevertheless, our thoughts do not compel us to action. Mentally healthy people are free to choose the actions they wish to implement. However, if we -as in the case of our unimplemented revenge- disregard our own anger, rage, or our helplessness in dealing with the experienced injustice and thus, what we are, others should be able to do so for us. Thus, we can accept the nature of man while rejecting his deeds.

Our personal being in the earthly humanity, which consists of our character, our temperament, and personality, underlies only very slightly our free will or our ability to make decisions. A large part thereof is bestowed upon us at birth. Another part of it is developed through education and socialization, as well as via witnessed or directly experienced suffering. We fully understand that people's experiences may cause serious internal issues and destroy not only their will and hope but also their moral values. Furthermore, these internal changes to thoughts and feelings following periods of physical or mental anguish may have serious consequences on the perception and experience of the person concerned. Dramatic and uncontrollable changes to one's personality may occur over time or in a few moments. No matter how much or compassion can address the suffering and ill-fated situation of those suffering or inflicting pain, it remains our task to distinguish between being and doing.

As long as we keep a clear mind, free of the influence of drugs or other substances, avoid specific illnesses such as psychosis, or are not violently forced by other people to perform certain actions, we should be fully accountable for our actions. Conversely, we are not for our feelings and thoughts.

Activation of the Soul Code
of Community

The second of our soul codes, the code of community, is freed and bubbles up as an inexhaustible source whenever we experience the following sentiments:

1. *We detract no energy from our fellow human beings.*

    Meeting other people is felt as a pleasant closeness. They thrive on the mutual contact and feel nourished and reinvigorated as we part. We may have given them our undivided attention or just met them for a fleeting instant. Whatever the case, they leave us with a pleasant, joyful feeling.

2. *We see ourselves in others.*

    We see all people as part of the community of souls. We are fully aware that we are all born as individual souls in earthly life, to learn and also to develop ourselves and help develop the community of souls.

3. *We distinguish between being and doing.*

We do not understand people for what they are but essentially for what they do.

Sick people may constitute an exception to this rule should the disease limit the ability to distinguish right from wrong, or impair or simply prevent freely chose actions.

To activate the code of community or to foster its development, it is especially important to recognize our fellow human beings as part of the community of souls and, therefore, part of us.

> ### Exercise for the code of community
>
> *Devote an entire day to go with fully open eyes through your life. Become consciously aware of every person you meet. For each one of them, say to yourself:*
>
> *"You too are a part of me."*
>
> *Beware if you find it overly easy, or if your statements lack real conviction at times. Repeat the exercise until you feel*

3

THE SOUL CODE OF RESONANCE

All earthly things are energy: all matter including plants, humans, or apparently inanimate nature. Underlying all formulas, molecular and cellular structures, minuscule findings or measurements, and every imaginable particle is always: Energy. Even our thoughts and feelings are made of energy. This view is essentially attributable to quantum physics, which has ultimately brought about quantum healing - probably without ever having to remember that healing could be a result of their observations. Meanwhile, this view has produced numerous insights and introduced new perspectives and opportunities for advancement in the spiritual paths of humanity. Understanding the energy and the use of its original form constitute major accomplishments. Anyhow, I would like to go slightly beyond this point. After all, energy is a very earthly phenomenon.

What can we learn from quantum physics? Does it reveal the soul code? - It may well do so, albeit in an understandable and appropriate secular way. It is part of our logical thinking to combine physical quantities with our humanity. Remarkably, it speaks of the everlasting human attempts to make Divinity scientifically comprehensible at last and explain and control the creative possibilities of our thoughts and desires by energy flow.

The law of resonance has been repeatedly described, receiving multiple introductions in religious teachings. Reduced to a simple formula, which is presented often as the universal and only rule of life, it states that we receive in our lives what we provide. However, I would like to go further because my spiritual experience requires so. The proponents of this universal and simple statement of faith often suggest that, anything beyond that would be only the expression of negative beliefs, unnecessarily complicating the simple way of success. Positive thinking and affirmative statements should be the easy way to happiness.

I agree with this approach in one particular point: There is a way to earthly happiness and to adequate wealth, which can manifest itself in material or financial prosperity. This does not necessarily require following a path of suffering and pain.

The wishing oracle often works. Expressed wishes come true in many cases while others remain unanswered. Now, why is it so? Were they wrongly formulated in the first place? Were the negative thoughts too strong? Maybe the constructive attitude energy was not held long enough? My answer is: The soul was not liberated! Its hidden code usually wanders around awaiting activation. Moreover, the question remains as to why the soul code is so well hidden. And why doesn't it activate by itself.

Each person comes to the world with learning tasks. It is the destiny of the soul to progressively evolve in the earthly world, learning new aspects with each life and thus moving forward. Souls are not identical. Even after earthly death, each soul is unique in its peculiarity. At the same time, the soul joins the community of other souls. It is not as limited as the human body is. You must not laboriously establish closeness and connection with other souls, because they already exist in the spiritual world. From an earthly standpoint, that is hard to imagine and all the metaphors and images that we can produce to understand the community of souls prove inadequate. Nevertheless, I will try to do so as only what we imagine can become reality. This also applies to the period after our earthly death, as we go across all of our religious beliefs and boundaries. In doing so, it opens up the vast expanse of universal and divine love and wisdom. It is entirely our decision to accept or reject it.

Let us imagine a huge swarm of fish moving in harmony. The impressive footage shows us this wonderful symphony of thousands of individual fish, which swarm together without any special agreement or common plan, while providing an overall result unattainable individually. It seems as though the swarm was endowed with a superior identity, that of a huge creature consisting of many moving cells. However, the positions within this collective present sometimes differing characteristics. For example, there are fodder favorable ones and those that offer increased protection. Some might allow a bit more or less free movement. In any case, each individual fish will benefit from the symphony of the swarm, its harmony, and the beauty of togetherness. Compared to the high level of soul-existence, we are like the fish rising in the communion of souls while still taking our own place, according to our own decisions.

We may understand that we swim in the soul swarm, or simply stay there, idly unaware. Just as it is possible to have individual dreams and beliefs, it is also possible to do so in the communion of souls. Note that our earthly existence is different. We seek other people's contact albeit we are not automatically associated with them. As a single stray fish that attempts to form small groups, we seek connection and security. The soul strives to restore its original state of connectedness. It is subject to the physical and psychological realities of this world. This desired state is attained only at a higher level, regardless of matter and logic. However, this is available for us now and here: It can be found in our mind. We can reach it in a mental fashion and thus open an eternal gateway to the spiritual world. Unfortunately, not every man will accomplish this in his current life. The ability to do so is nonetheless self-created in each one of us. Those who manage to initiate the activation of their soul code in a conscious manner will achieve such goal as well.

Here, the law of resonance plays a decisive role. It does not mean, however, as it is usually described, that we receive in our life what we provide. It is also irrelevant what we think or what our beliefs are. Similarly, it does not rest on our good or evil intentions or a moral development. The truth is, we do not always receive in our lives what we provide. Thousands of disappointed people find that their well-formulated and positively-worded wishes unfulfilled. Despite all the reprogramming of negative beliefs through positive formulas and intense auto-suggestions, many motivated people fail and look for the causes.

In physics, the idea of resonance states that an energy vibration creates another one. Now, while it is possible to describe physical laws, I have already stressed that the soul is not subject to these. It is not made of energy. It has a much more divine form of existence, which our human understanding could hitherto only describe by stating that the soul *is*. It does exist. It exists and it outlasts everything.

The wishes we send into the universe or to the spiritual world are not conveyed as energy. The path of submission as well as its origin is the soul. It is true that every wish can also be fulfilled. It does not depend, however, on the rituals or faith but on the nature of the soul. Therefore, we apply what corresponds to the state and thus to the development of our soul. However, this is something other than the na-

ture of thought and action. Thinking and acting
- even feeling - are easily trainable and can be
simply conditioned. Our basic attitude correlates although not permanently to the state of
our soul. In the first part of this book, I did
show that humans tend to repress their own
feelings in the short term, change them in the
medium term, and abandon them in the long-
term to please other people. To experience
their attention and benevolent affection for as
long as possible. From our earliest childhood,
we give up the connection to our soul in favor
of earthly gratification. As adults, we are "self-
weaned" and often think we know only what
we feel and think deep inside. In courses and
therapies, meditations, and religious communi-
ties, we attempt to build up other attitudes,
feelings, and ideas that will make us a better
person in our own eyes. Even so, we can then
take ideas and concepts of others without pay-
ing attention to how our true state appears. But
this is precisely what matters, because wishes
come true when they are in harmony with our
true state and thus again, with the development
of the soul. Therefore, it is important to discover and be fully aware of one's own soul
while enabling its development. A fully liberated soul, which activates its code in this life,

develops without effort by itself and in harmony with divine wisdom. It leaves no desires unfulfilled without even having to formulate them. The status of the soul makes true what correlates to its development. How we deal with ourselves and with our life reflects such status.

At this point, we should necessarily consider the question of how long it takes for a person to develop his soul, to the point that his wishes are consistent with it. Here, we require an approach of higher abstraction than the earthly view of things. Frequently, certain sought-after "big" desires, such as earning a fortune, are not really that important. After our death, we shall be solely measured by how much love we leave behind in the world. Love is the greatest contribution we can make to humanity and this requires a high soul development level. How far should a soul progress in its development in order to obtain a fortune per wish request? - Not as far as most people might think: Human life on earth is primarily created to apprehend the nature of the soul and unleash its creative and loving force. No minor feat. If one succeeds in activating the soul code and liberating the four individual soul codes, doing so in a conscious and fully aware fashion, then everything else happens by itself. The perpetual motion machine, -a machine that rotates constantly with no influx of energy or energy consumption- sought after for centuries by scientists to no avail, already exists. It is the soul. It lies nonetheless dormant during our earthly life. It is waiting to be liberated, to be allowed to unfold in its beauty and harmony. The relevant code is within each one of us. Discovering and unleashing it is our life's work.

Quantum healing is based on the contact with the pure consciousness (or to the pure consciousness), which is also called "awareness". The users of quantum healing leverage the development of the most original of all energies, and thus bring about a harmonization of the human organism and the activation of unprecedented self-healing abilities. Thus, they take place very close to the soul. For behind the pure consciousness, beyond this energy - playing in a state where energy is irrelevant -, there is the soul. We cannot establish the connection just with pure awareness. The fathers of quantum healing describe in a vivid and edifying manner how easy it is to do so. The value humanity may derive from its access to this energy source is immense. The beautiful and adventurous journey inviting us to the quantum healing continues. In fact, you can reach even the world beyond pure consciousness - that is, the world of the soul.

The liberated and code-activated soul unfolds by itself. It leverages all the magic to help it grow and restore its original soul status. It will automatically bring abundance and prosperity to our earthly life. And every soul-liberating wish will be fulfilled.

Joshua and the Angel of Earth - Part 3

After one of Joshua's deaths, he met again the Angel of Earth to discuss about his past life. He had many questions, but felt particularly concerned with the envy he had experienced in great measure.

"Angel of Earth, why is it that human envy, this cold and cruel trait, overtook me so frequently in my past life?"

As it happened upon each Joshua's return to the spiritual world of the community of souls, the Angel of Earth answered his questions. He knew that Joshua had been a successful and respected man in his past life. He also knew that he frequently felt jealousy and resentment.

"Tell me, Joshua", the Angel of Earth said, "did envy win you at anytime?"

"I felt no envy whatsoever", was Joshua's answer.

"So, how come you believed others were jealous of you?"

"So many turned away from me when I was successful. They even crossed the street when they saw me. They talked about me behind closed doors. What else could that be but jealousy and resentment? "

"Joshua, I am surprised how suspicious you're grown," said the Angel of Earth. And he continued: "How did you react? What did you do to reach out to your fellow human beings? What did you do to understand what they really thought of you? "

Joshua answered: "I did nothing in that respect. I thought it better to distance myself from their envy and follow my own path. Angel of Earth, you did advice me once not to seek reconciliation with those who oppose me or do me wrong. Should I assume that is no longer the case?"

"You still do not understand, don't you, Joshua? Do you really ignore why you encountered such envy again and again?" the angel asked.

"Yes, I do not know why that happened" Joshua answered.

"What would have shown you", the angel asked further, "that they were not jealous, but maybe simply insecure?"

"Had they reached out to me without reservations, I would have seen that it was not envy they felt. In such case, I may have wanted to understand what they really felt."

"Hence, it was the silence between you that produced such scenario" said the Angel of Earth.

"Yes, indeed" answered Joshua although he did not understand what the Angel or Earth actually meant.

"Although you made no effort to break such silence" continued the Angel of Earth. "You withdrew from them, sometimes you even hid in your own house so that they could not see you. You were peering through the window just to see their skeptical gaze confirm your own image of people's envies. Like them, you only spoke behind closed doors. What would you say they had in mind? "

Joshua considered the question. In his memory he could see himself again. He felt again the angry loneliness he had felt in his recurring self-pity. Joshua began to understand and turned to the Angel of Earth. He was waiting patiently for Joshua to realize that this supposed envy was like a mirror into which he frequently gazed.

"They probably saw me just as I saw them. I believe my reticence and caution had made me appear aloof and strange to them. My character may have even bittered as a result. Perhaps they have taken me for a man envious of those satisfied albeit less successful in life. Tell me, Angel of Earth, was that the price I had to pay for my worldly success?"

"Of course not" the angel replied. "As you know, there is neither reward nor punishment or any form of price for what you are on earth. It is just that, in your earthly life, you will be shown especially that which correlates to the state of your soul."

"Was there really nothing else?" asked Joshua. "How come I could not enjoy honesty or friendship? Was my stubborn soul a hindrance to that end?"

Even if the soul code lies broken and slumbers waiting for redemption deep within us, we may still submit our wishes: to the universe, to the spiritual world, or to God and the angels. All these goals describe the same instance. They will be attained as they become relevant to our soul development. As long as wish fulfillment is of use to us, they will activate the code of our soul and light the fire of its development. However, this is not always so. Should we live against the original code of the soul and therefore in opposition to creation that brought our souls forward, the fulfillment of a material or a spiritual desire could become more a curse than a blessing for us. To be sure, wishing for a millionaire profit to distribute it amongst poor people may be regarded as an honorable act. Then again, would such profit rekindle the soul code of the wisher? – The answer to this question is the decision criterion for wish fulfillment. Therefore, it is irrelevant to become or remain an honorable man on our wish fulfillment purposes but for us to foster our full soul development. Our soul is never completely inactive. As we have already seen in the previously described code, it is always striving to restore its original state. It starts its journey home with the first breath of the newborn.

Soul code 3

In our earthly life, we consider events and circumstances that reflect the state of our soul.

The highest development of the human soul would be the achievement of the soul state of the spiritual world on earth. That is precisely what our souls seek to attain in every earthly life. Wish fulfillment does not depend on the degree of achievement of this goal but solely on the extent of additional development said fulfillment provides to the soul code. A soul that lives half asleep and fails to correctly release its code due to earthly limitations, will remain in such state through material wishes.

Activation of the Soul Code of Resonance

The third soul code, the Code of Resonance, is freed and bubbles up as an inexhaustible source, whenever we experience the following sentiments:

1. ***We recognize the connection between the building blocks of our life.***

   Looking back on our life, we suddenly and recurrently realize that all phases of our earthly life intertwine in a special way while it dawns upon us that everything had to be exactly how we experienced it.

2. ***We recognize ourselves in the current events of our lives.***

   We realize that the events that befall us seemingly at random are like an echo of our emotional state. We understand the relationship between failure or stagnation and our attitude. Conversely, we feel successes and other positive events not as grandiose coincidences anymore but as appropriate and consistent events.

3. **We meet more like-minded people.**

   We feel that we are surrounded by many people with similar thoughts. We constantly meet new people who appear to be familiar although we have not met them before.

Needless to say, we always meet people that match our own state of mind. Our unbridled soul code makes this suddenly appear as providential. We now acknowledge the similarity of these people to us and realize our meeting is no random event.

To activate or further develop the code of resonance, it is especially important to find the reflection of our soul in the events of our lives.

> ***Exercise for the code of resonance***
>
> *Write down on separate pieces of paper each significant event of your life from the following four areas: family life, school, work, and friendship. For each area, write down a pleasant and an un-*

pleasant experience. Look at all of them individually and say:

"That was a reflection of my soul."

Now, answer the following questions:

What part of me was actually reflected in that event?
What did I learn from that experience?

You should always approach this exercise considering that neither pleasant events do occur by way of reward nor unpleasant or unfair events occur by way of punishment from the Universe. Try to recall and acknowledge your soul state as the event happened. Then, consider what you did learn. This is not about actions triggered by a particular event but about self-discovery. Finally, list the internal conclusion you have drawn.

4

THE SOUL CODE OF KARMA

"Karma" is a nebulous, poorly defined concept because it has been adopted by representatives of multiple faiths with different meanings and purposes. Since I intend to use it, I would like to first explain my understanding of the term. My concern is neither to provide yet another "Karma" definition nor to reject any meanings non-adhering thereto. Admittedly, the relationships that I will describe hereby could certainly be expressed using different terms. However, my name for them is Karma.

We tend to place the events of our lives in a relationship of cause and effect. Most people understand, however, that all our actions introduce changes. Their effect may go from the inconspicuous to the certainly evident and even produce and impressive and lasting impact. Regardless, there are instances in which our earthly understanding fails to fathom the sense underlying certain events or find the cause for numerous life events. Nevertheless, there is the contingency of the physical world - those higher-level connections, which state that all earthly existence is energy and this is always interacting with other energies. Ultimately, all earthly things, whether matters or thoughts, stem from this force. Energy is not lost but transformed.

Hence, nothing of what we think or do is inconsequential. The consequences of our actions often appear as huge boulders on the path of our life and must be laboriously rolled to the side. At times, people endure the life-long consequences of their actions. It also occurs naturally, that our decisions and actions produce a positive effect of which we benefit. All demands and challenges in life, be it the difficult or the easy ones, befall us for one reason only: As learning tasks, they should make us aware of the nature of our soul and help us live our purpose: the liberation and development of our soul and the activation of our soul codes. That's it. On the one hand, it appears as a simple and clearly defined task while, on the other hand, it constitutes the biggest challenge humanity has to face. All religions of the world describe the learning or development activities of human beings. These differ significantly content-wise. Common to all of them is the effort to reconcile the learning tasks with the divine wisdom and with purpose of the soul. Behind all the cultural and civilization-shaped ideas, whose content human learning tasks might well adopt, there is only one task to be fulfilled: self-liberation.

To that end, we may follow two paths: Patiently, step by step, we can wait for the challenges of daily life, accept them and try to master them. This requires earthly actions and spiritual confrontations. In case we fall from a ladder and break a leg, we will have to face the pain and provide appropriate treatment so that our daily life continues to function. We plan and organize. All the things we cannot do while our leg is broken can either remain undone or be assigned to an assistant for execution. At the same time, we will hopefully find some peace to think things over. We might ask ourselves, what learnings or eventual benefits we may derive from a broken leg. For example, we may consider what we should do differently in the future to avoid such risks. More importantly, a broken leg offers us a few days opportunity to come closer to our own and thus liberate our soul code. Sometimes we succeed, sometimes we do not. Life is full of small and big challenges - painful albeit also pleasant. Making the ladder more stable and slip-safe is nearly irrelevant for the activation of mental codes. Conversely, learning to use this daily life interruption for self-reflection, freeing our feelings again, meditating, praying, or simply experiencing silence, will see the well of our soul code bubbling up and us taking advantage of the learning task. Fortunately, our leg does not break twenty times in a row - not even if we fail to leverage the event. We are continuously offered learning opportunities. Every day.

The second path is one of a decidedly active nature: the path of understanding and acceptance. Even before the next challenge appears in the horizon, we can see to the liberation of our soul. Every day, as we attempt to free our internal, call-awaiting soul code and rekindle the fire of its development, the soul begins to unfold itself. It continuously seeks an ever greater development. All we need is to live consciously every day. We can begin every day in the consciousness of the soul codes and attempt to feel their influence. It is easier than we usually imagine. Check it out for yourselves, dear readers. Can you relate to my comments? Can you feel how your soul code begins to bubble up upon reading? There is no need to do anything special. There is no need for a ritual or an affirmation. Anchor the existence of the soul codes into your consciousness. And soon begins its development and continues on. Every new day.

Learning tasks do not demand from us to draw any substantive lessons from particular events. They constitute neither punishment nor reward for our lifestyle or our deeds. They should allow our self-knowledge and the knowledge of our soul status. This can be an almost comatose sleep period or a dance of unbridled harmony - or one of the countless possibilities lying in between.

Let us deal with the unfolding of the soul as we accept the soul code so our live can flow and proceed on earthly wealth and prosperity or how it correlates with our personal wishes. As long as the soul code remains active, we approach to the original form of our existence and live in harmony with creation.

Nothing in life happens by chance. All encounters are part of a divine plan. This is always created to lead us to our true destiny. It goes beyond the mere liberation of our soul. Such step is just the beginning. In the end, it is also about the community of souls. The development of the individual through his developed soul code contributes to the advancement of all humanity. In each human being lives a soul out of the large community from which we come. However, we do not live on Earth all at once. Many souls present in the spiritual world are repeatedly born to learn on Earth. Thus, a part of all souls is found in earthly life and another in the spiritual world. Someday, however, all souls will be reunited. This will not happen on the day the Earth goes down and the Last Judgment day looms. It will be the day when humanity reaches the he spiritual world state in its overall development, where all souls live according to the destiny of their soul codes. From our current vantage point, this idea may well be considered mere wishful-thinking and an utopic proposition. It is, however, the destination of humanity, the goals of the community of souls and their common journey. More and more people will understand the soul code over time and accept it. As their souls leave their dormant state, these people bring their ever growing love to the world. They send them out because they are then in a state of Love. They take others along on the journey and enable their soul code through the purity of their love. They bring humanity closer to the spiritual world and both become increasingly similar until they eventually merge into one another.

However, man is not completely open and willing to learn about the world. In fact, he does not enter the earthly existence as a blank slate or approaches the world at ease. We add a lot to this earthly life. We call it character, personality, temperament, and talent. All these human aspects are changeable, can be developed or attenuated over time. In any case, there is always something present from birth. We can persuade ourselves that is brought along with our genes and the result of heredity. Indeed, that may be true from a worldly perspective. If we consider it from a higher vantage point, we remind ourselves that all matter and ultimately all energy in this world is only an earthly manifestation of the soul-existence. Our genes reflect only what our soul gave the human corset for our earthly life.

Our learnings in each earthly life spare the soul the corresponding experience. Even though that is a common belief, we ask ourselves where such knowledge remains and how come we repeatedly lose it, so we need to start learning from scratch in the next life. This question, however, is not a valid one: We do not lose our learnings. Only the content of our experiences disappears. We will not need it in any way in another life. That we have really fathomed and learned remains eternal. We bring it as a character, personality, temperament and talent to the world. These qualities dictate the starting point of our earthly self-development. They are more or less suited to activate the soul code. If our innate basic properties become a self-detrimental preoccupation, attaining the soul code liberation becomes a difficult and tortuous path. For example, we may born as profound thinkers, displaying a highly developed interest in the meaning of life already in childhood, so we quickly recognize and initiate the soul codes activation.

However, our development opportunities are not predetermined from birth. God's greatest gift is free will. Every day, He gives us the opportunity to stand up and set a new course. Regardless of whether our soul code is in deep sleep or bursting with live upon birth, we can activate it every day and turn into an ever burning fire. If we set our code free or help it up to a higher level as we unleash it and let it flow, our development continues daily and we attain everything we deem important. This includes worldly goals and conveniences. They come all alone in our life when the soul code unfolds.

Furthermore, every day of our earthly life we are offered opportunities to see, recognize, accept, and liberate this code. We can be aware of its existence and foster it every day. The message states: Experience the principle of creation! It lives within us and is expressed through the soul code. We can live it every day.

Who determines the tasks we encounter in life? Who determines which events will help us to understand and fully develop the human and soul existences? Who determines our karma? - That is precisely what I mean by "karma": the selection of our learning tasks. Once again, I should point out that I do not intend to claim the concept of karma for my teaching. I will use the term in the way described hereby, being far from my intention to spark any disputes with other religious approaches using the term differently. Karma is understood by most people as a part of oneself that is carried over to a next life. That is the meaning of the term I am using.

Therefore, when we ask ourselves why certain events happen in our lives, while encountering karmic causes, our worldly thoughts slip quickly into the idea of a divine rule. Negative events are then often perceived as a form of punishment for the sins of a past life. Conversely, experiences of success are considered as rewards for previous acts of high moral value of a past life. As plausible as this idea might seem, it reduces the divine wisdom to the jurisdiction of Hammurabi, who as king of Babylonia draw up the Codex Hammurabi nearly four thousand years ago, including the legal principle of "an eye for an eye, a tooth for a tooth". Suppose a man was shot by a bank robber and came with the idea of karma in contact. He would probably conclude that he had inflicted and injury in a previous life and therefore would have to endure now that karma. From an energy point of view, a balance would be created. His soul may also draw a lesson and his soul code may become increasingly active through its confrontation. Now, the "offender" could keep in store the same thing pursuant to this idea. Either in the current or in the next life he would have to reckon with an injury inflicted on him by another as compensation for the wrongs committed on himself.

Amazingly enough, every idea of humanity is missing here. Earthly civilized societies have long since distanced themselves from such re taliation of misconduct. Numerous representatives of such simple karma teachings condemn such a direct way of answering behavior on earth, while still consider this karma-retribution for a portion of the divine plan. Humanity has long considered it a mark of its moral development to overcome the inhumane legal philosophy of Hammurabi. God is, however, well ahead of us, we can be sure. He does not require a retribution system of this sort.

Soul code 4

The human soul brings into the earthly life self-selected, specially imposed learning tasks, which we unfulfilled in a previous life.

Learning tasks, which include also the terrible events or suffering from wrongdoings, come upon us neither as rewards nor punishments for the deeds of a previous life. These are inscribed in the book of our life before birth. Therefore, we can hardly ignore them. Nevertheless, our lives are not entirely predetermined. We should decide how we deal with the learning tasks, what lessons we draw from them and how these apply to our earthly life.

The book of life has many blank pages, which we will fill in the course of earthly existence. However, some are already full and contain our responsibilities. These are geared towards a single goal: They allow us to recognize the soul codes. They force us to activate the silent potential of the soul codes dormant within us. If we seize this opportunity, we have already completed the learning task. However, if we ignore the opportunity because we do not perceive it as such, the next learning task enters soon into our lives and requires us to follow our destiny once again. Hence, each chapter in the book of our life contains numerous learning tasks of varied expressiveness. Let us consider the first or the second, perhaps even up to the tenth one, and feel their soul development values so we may spare the rest. We actively occupy ourselves with the soul code and our humanity, developing the code in doing so without the need for further learning tasks.

The full pages in the book of our live will be deleted. In doing so, we will end with an open and blank book, which we can fill with our own wishes and dreams. It no longer matters whether this is worldly desire or spiritual enlightenment. We are experiencing the principle of creation! This most original of all the tasks makes any other superfluous. Happiness and abundance enter our lives. Without affirmation, without expressed desires, and for no consideration.

Joshua and the Angel of Earth - Part 4

Joshua met the Angel of Earth because he wished to be born again as a human being.

"Angel of Earth, please do send me to Earth one more time. I would like to re-learn and achieve a deeper understanding of my soul. "

The Angel of Earth, entrusted with sending souls, opened the book of life, which was ready for Joshua.

"Tell me Joshua, what will you learn in your next life?"

"I want to learn to forgive. Enjoy opportunities to forgive other people. If I succeed, I will overcome the earthly interests of vengeance, the human feelings of hatred, and make my soul development possible."

The Angel of Earth smiled and replied: "You know that forgiveness is only relevant if you carry at the same time a deep feeling inside that one you wronged. One that is irreparable. Anything else would not be forgiveness, Joshua. Forgiveness for something not leading to severe life degradation or whenever the offender meant actually good cannot be considered actual forgiveness."

"But what else could that be?" Joshua asked, confused.

"It is the result of your consideration, a representation of your assessment of whether a balance of energy has occurred. If you want to learn to forgive, you should try it without the remorse of the offender. Are you ready, Joshua?"

"What should I do? Should I be his friend? Maybe even help him or do him some good, although he may keep on causing me pain and suffering?"

"Not really, Joshua", replied the angel, "there is no need to be a martyr on earth to that end. You are free to pursue martyrdom if you wish to do so. However, no one is asking from you such a sacrifice. There is no need for you to follow a common path with your tormentor. You may want to forgive - thus attempt to drop the hate that you will build to endure the injustice. Try to find your inner peace and under-

stand your tormentors as part of the community of souls. Find the destination of your soul through the experience that you will undergo together. Ignite the code of your soul existence by freeing yourself from thoughts of vengeance and bad wishes for these people. If you manage to wish him all the best in your thoughts and avoid any grief over the thought that he could live successfully in spite of their actions and content, then you have fulfilled the task. For then, dear Joshua, your soul will be unleashed. There is no need to allow these people into your life again. You can ban him from it as the togetherness is fulfilled. Concern yourself, if so is your wish, with preventing any further contact with him. Living, however, without hate and thoughts of revenge while feeling your own development. Tell me now, Joshua: Are you ready? "

"Yes, I will try to do so. Although I ignore whether I am already so far. "

"It was one of your tasks. Nonetheless, there is something else you need to accomplish. As you well know, the divine wisdom entrusted you with as tasks in your earthly life. The divine purpose of your next life will be that of charity. Hence, you will have the opportunity

to act mercifully. This task will be presented repeatedly until you feel ready to accept it. Finally, Joshua, there is a third task. It comes from your last earthly life. This is one you did not embrace. For this reason, your soul could not develop as much as you desired. Moreover, this task is still unfulfilled. It was the challenge of letting go. There were so many things you had to let go externally in your past life. Internally, however, you did not succeed in doing so. So take this task again along with your journey. At time, it will seem as if you were persecuted by fate. If you manage to experience the soul code, you will realize that your destiny -or your karma, as you will call it on earth- is an expression of your yet unfulfilled tasks. Thus, take these three task types along: those you chose, those divinely provided, and those unfulfilled."

Activation of the Soul Code
of Karma

The fourth soul code, the Code of Karma, is freed and bubbles up as an inexhaustible source, whenever we experience the following sentiments:

1. *We recognize the great themes of life as tasks.*

   We no longer make statements such "I always have bad luck" or "Why is this happening to me?" In fact, we do not even think that way. We just understood that evil does not haunt us but we are simply offered unresolved tasks once again. Even in very awkward situations, we try to understand difficulties as tasks than we may have selected ourselves at some point before our earthly birth. Certainly, we may nonetheless experience doubt at times, seeing discrimination or punishment therein. At least, however, we attempt to understand karma.

2. *We feel that we are not helpless in
    the fact of fate.*

    *Karma is inevitable. Therefore, there are
    certain events, themes or problems we
    simply cannot handler or omit. How-
    ever, we feel ever more often that pre-
    cisely the inevitable, be it pleasant or
    unpleasant, contains the challenge of
    acting. Learning happens beyond our
    thoughts. The process of learning and its
    results are visible in our decisions and
    deeds. As Codes are activated, the
    statement "Nothing is so bad that noth-
    ing good can come out of it" appears
    truly meaningful.*

3. *We seek the highest possible spiri-
    tual development.*

    *Dealing with karmic issues puts you al-
    ready en route to an interesting spiri-
    tual development. An activated karma
    code will inevitably mean that we seek
    an ever deeper spiritual knowledge and
    thus a higher level of spiritual develop-
    ment. The intellectual and meditative
    study of the spiritual world, the con-
    tinuous attempt of understanding and*

communication with those in it with
light beings or angels souls, belong to
our karma-activated lives.

To activate or further develop the code of karma it is especially important to recognize the recurring themes of our lives as karmic responsibilities and to accept them as such.

Exercise of the code of karma

Think about what issues and difficulties you encounter repeatedly. You may acknowledge that you have had similar difficulties with different life partners. You may have probably experienced the curse of jealousy or dependence, typically in connection with personal relationships. Furthermore, you may have already experienced several professional difficulties or have fallen repeatedly in similar moral conflicts. You probably know the recurring patterns of certain experiences. In this exercise, note also the typical schemes that you have encountered repeatedly in the areas of family, work, and friendship.

Take each note and read what it says. Then say:

"My soul has chosen itself this topic as a learning opportunity"

Then, answer the following questions about the topic:

What I can learn from this topic?
How can I let it go?

Then say again, "My soul has chosen itself this topic as a learning opportunity" and note whether you find it easy or if you sometimes fail to say it with conviction. Repeat the exercise until you feel confident about uttering such statement, even when dealing with painful experiences. Keep in mind you do not have to agree with other person's deeds.

PART III

THE CREATION CONTINUES

SEVEN DAYS SHALL NOT SUFFICE

The Christian creation story tells us how God created the world in seven days. Admittedly, not many people believe today in the absolute truth of this idea. The scientific theory of evolution has repeatedly tried to answer the question of the origins of man without reference to a divine creation. For all living things, their development path is fraught with increasing uncertainty the farther we look into the past. The question whether man evolved from a single-celled marine organism or was sent as God's child on Earth separates evolutionary considerations from religious ideas and may stay on earth forever unanswered. The existence of the spiritual world and thus the existence of the soul after death is currently no longer a matter of religious belief. An ever increasing number of people have an intuitive approach to this world, receive messages from it or communicate with their souls. Their information and reports are disseminated through the modern media world and prove difficult to ignore. In recent years, solely through the introduction of books dealing with the spiritual world and the human condition, millions of people have gained access to spirituality. This book may prove a valuable contribution to the spiritual development of those readers who find precisely on this journey.

Creation is not a unique occurrence. The world in which we live was not created as our gift or for us to destroy. We are not the children of a closed creation story. *We* are the creation. Here, the evolution is reconciled with the idea of the human children of God. The entire nature evolves continuously under the threat of human exploitation and its destructive use. Nonetheless, humanity is also evolving. The more people activate their soul codes, the higher level of spiritual development they may attain. We become increasingly similar to our original form. We are driving the creation forward. We develop it further. In other words: The creation is fulfilled by the human search for meaning through the development of the human soul. The people living today are able to enjoy intellectual and spiritual benefits that a thousand years ago were not even possible. In another thousand years, we will have achieved an even higher level of abstraction. However, this does not affect all people in equal measure. Those who are ahead of their time and have already achieved a high level of spiritual development will lead others, who are taken away by the love of the "mastermind" to this higher level.

Creation itself was not completed in seven days. It is an ongoing process. Our search for meaning and the liberation of our soul progressively fulfills the divine creation. The aim of creation is to attain on earth the soul state of the spiritual world. The separation between earthly and spiritual life in the spiritual world will then disappear. Let start our journey and become aware of our soul codes every day. To know and forever feel how our soul progressively unfolds brings us closer to the summit of creation every day. By activating our soul code daily or feeling how it continuously develops after activation, we amply serve the creation and live in wealth, prosperity, contentment, and happiness. The success comes all by itself in our earthly life, in the form of wealth, recognition, and security. Moreover, we gain spiritual success in terms of creativity and trust, closeness to the spiritual world and to the souls living therein, which are always among us. The message of the spiritual world is: Experience the principle of creation! It is within the soul code waiting for liberation!

MAN AS EXECUTOR OF CREATION

The constant movement of evolution, the development of living beings and even the seemingly inanimate nature puts the real, unfinished story of creation before us every day. It happens every day, every hour, and every minute. New life forms continuously emerge. Deep in the oceans, cell structures arise under the light of creation as new living creatures. Conversely, other living creatures die and leave the path of creation. Quantum physics teaches us that nothing is lost. All matter is ultimately energy, subsiding even after death.

The creation uses such energy. It is the basis of its earthly development. Nonetheless, creation is far more than an energy equilibrium effort. Our mind can go much deeper and further than it would be necessary to understand the notion of a primal energy or quantum energy. We may even discover soul is not made of energy. Its existence is described by terrestrial standards only approximately. The real dimensions of the soul, its existence without energy, may overwhelm our minds. However, we are aware of the soul by experiencing the soul code, as it affects us on a level far above that which energy is able to provide: It stands in direct connection to the spiritual world where the community of souls reside.

Mediums, which are in contact with the spiritual world, report regularly of special energetic processes. Indeed, dead souls need energy to engage with us. Using modern methods of measurement, such energy can be captured and even made partially visible. However, this has to do solely with the fact that we live in a material and thus energy-based world. The spiritual world itself does not require any energy. For its form of existence is independent of any physical conditions. To be sure, this may disturb or seem even impossible to certain quantum physicists. Nevertheless, such world is not built upon energy. This idea corresponds solely to our mere earthly minds.

Evolution always seeks further development. Man, as the earthly creature with the largest active influence on events, lives every day the divine providence and the plan of creation. However, one might ask: Is man the epitome of development or, conversely, is he to become the destroyer of his own world?

Humanity leaves good but also evil in its wake. Wars, economic interests, and religious differences have regularly brought destruction to the world. In the last twenty years, natural disasters and climate change have shown us the time has come to leave the beaten path of earthly concerns behind and continue to walk the path of creation. Once again, however, none of these events carry the punishment or revenge of the universe or a divine instance. They simply point to our task: discovering the human soul, its liberation, and the life of creation.

All too often, man is described as the destroyer of the world and in its apparent stupidity, is placed in the exact center of the pillory. The very existence of humanity is no accident of nature. We are the executors of evolution. Every day, the creation is fulfilled and continued in and through us. The creation continues! The task of maintaining nature while handling its resources in a respectful and dignified manner and caring for animals as part of God's earthly plan, constitute essential components of the creation idea. Our planet is the earthly world in which we were born to fulfill the creation. The aim of creation is the journey home to our original soul-existence. To that end, we develop our souls and become wiser to provide and ever growing contribution to the advance of the spiritual world community. Because even these souls learn and evolve. They too live the creation. Even in the spiritual world, there are less active and liberated souls. For after our earthly death, we shall indeed enjoy the infinite love and wisdom of this world, although the activation of the soul codes is still up to us then.

The Day of Judgment will not be the ending point of human history. It will be this one, very special day, where the earthly and the spiritual worlds openly encounter to finally merge. All earthly souls will leave the physical enclosure of their bodies and their environment and achieve the state of existence that souls in the spiritual world hold before and after our earthly life. With each earthly life, we initiate the journey home of the soul. Besides the personal task of soul evolution and the liberation of our soul codes, there is also a collective mission for humankind: This lies in the evolution of the community of souls. For our earthly existence, this means the development of humanity at large. It is not about technical progress or compensating inequalities in the distribution of resources. It has more to do with the common evolution to a higher level of soul development. Souls in the spiritual world exist simultaneously in their individuality and in union with the community of souls. On Earth, however, our personality and our physicality are separated. Now, the eventual encounter of the earthly world with the spiritual one, which we consider as a goal of earthly creation, can only happen if humanity has fulfilled the creation. Not all people will develop in equal measure. Differences in attitudes, beliefs, moral or ethical values are irrelevant. Only the state of souls, the extent of their liberation and development of soul codes determines when humanity can achieve the goal of creation.

The question is: when will that day come? Is the goal of creation maybe achieved when all souls in their earthly existence attain the highest level of soul development? Are we all bound to be reborn again until the last soul has reached such state?

This will probably not be the case. Not all souls are the same age. Even if there is no time left in the spiritual world, we may still find numerous souls who have lived only a few times on earth. Conversely, others would have had numerous earthly existences. Young souls do not live in a distinct spirituality. They are subject to the earthly, advantage-seeking material things. New souls, born for the first time in an earthly existence, keep coming back. They show us the necessity of the common path. Our encounters with them require us to undertake the task of our own development but also that of the entire mankind. The promotion of creation is one of the goals of highly-developed souls. Through the development of one's own soul and the associated transmission of love and charity, through this unselfish contribution to the welfare of the community of souls, we create the basis for the transition of humanity into the spiritual world.

As most of us feel ready to understand and accept the tasks of our earthly existence, to live the further evolution of one's soul through the development of the soul code as the most original of all provisions, the community of these souls will become like Noah's Ark for all those who cannot take this route by themselves. Needless to say, I cannot calculate how many souls meeting the creation goal would be necessary to build this ark of humanity. Regardless, the more engaged in activating the soul code and living the principle of creation, the closer we come to this great creation goal: the fusion of the earthly with the spiritual world.

WISHES COME TRUE

It is human nature to seek "the" happiness. This eternal search has been sung about in songs, described in literature, and represented in numerous plays. Many stories have been written about persons seeking happiness in earthly wealth at the outset to eventually find a philosophical revelation: happiness that is independent of material conditions. In fact, we seek something beyond what earth can offer us. At the same time, we are not independent of material circumstances in our lifetime. The desire for reasonable abundance in this world is therefore justified and does not contradict the plan of creation. Strictly speaking, material conditions play no role in the state of our soul. This seeks the journey back to its place of origin and to connect with the community of souls in the spiritual world. Therefore, our earthly existence is just a transit station, as a visit to a school in which we could and should develop our potential. It is our mission to unleash the soul code and thus to live the principle of creation. If we manage to do so, all material wealth and prosperity will come by itself in our earthly life. We will become successful, evidencing with our wishes what the state of our soul on earth represents: Growth!

The fulfillment of material wishes will suppress our soul code if this is already half asleep. If we can barely experience or feel the four soul codes as I describe them hereby, these will lie inoperative, unable to contribute to their own soul development and thus to the creation. Tens of millions in our bank account would only make things worse. A wise man once said, money does not spoil the character, just brings its to the forefront. I concur. We often see examples of people who suddenly come into money, be it through inheritance, lottery winnings, or otherwise, which seem to become very unpleasant or arrogant contemporaries. We do not recognize them anymore. After a few years past, the wealth is gone. Most of them are poorer now than they were after the riches. Were these people too careless? Were they stupid or just inexperienced? Did they engage the wrong advisor? Did money change them? Could they have behaved differently?

Beyond the earthly search for an explanation, we may find two answers at the soul level. Either the person has abandoned the soul code and thus violated the creation or he has "turned off" the active code. In the first case, the lottery money could have been considered as a learning task. It entered a person's life to offer him an opportunity to learn something, for example, to become a helper that does not provide material assistance albeit emotional support. Now, if this man, a lucky lottery winner, cares for the development of his soul and can uncover, recognize, and activate the soul code, he will live the creation while keeping his wealth. He would have fulfilled his task. Let us always remember that behind the content of learning tasks stands the need for the soul code activation. Doing so guarantees the learning task fulfillment.

Now, how is it possible to shut down an already activated and living soul code again or to largely suppress it? Creation has given us an important instrument for dealing with ourselves and the world around us: free will. We can always choose to serve the creation or separate ourselves from it. Our soul code is constantly evolving. Let us consider the code of love: It will take us some time to liberate ourselves from other people's views and let them be who they truly are. For humans, this is a great task we should only approach in a gradual manner. We succeed through practice and self-clarification although only sometimes or just partly at the beginning. Over time, we increasingly feel that we can forgive others and avoid judging them for what they are. In its highest development, we remain completely free of judgments about the nature of others.

However, our free will allows losing ground on our development. In fact, we can undermine an already attained level for an individual code or for all codes of the human soul. For the earthly existence constantly challenges us to think and act according to the state of our soul. Thus, if the level attained for a given code is not stable enough, it may be lost, forcing us to start over again. A certain person may enjoy being easy-going and non-judgmental in many situations. At the same time, there may be situations this person finds extremely difficult or unrealizable. Earthly wealth could allow this man to avoid this particular challenge in the future. A few days before the event, the lottery winner may ask himself why it is so difficult for him to endure certain people even though they did him no wrong. Then, one day after the winnings are published, he may consider that some people do not deserve better. So, what did happen? - He made a decision: the free choice to think and act exactly at this level, even though he once wanted to actually develop it further. At such a moment, he "turns off" the code of love or freezes it in the first place. However, the level already attained is gradually lost. At this point, there are two paths he can follow: Love for those who deserve it and misunderstanding for those who do not. A landmark ruling on whether the individual is included in the scope of charity. The destruction of the code has begun.

The good news is that we can start in anytime during our lifetime to experience our soul code again. It is never too late to embrace it. The more we do so, the sooner and more clearly will wealth enter our lives. For our soul is able to handle it and allow that thought and thus the reality of wealth. Therefore, our wishes may come true. It is not dependent of the formulation or the type of programming or affirmation, but solely on whether the wish-fulfillment fosters our soul code. In the described example, the speech was about the specific learning task of the lottery winnings. Such tasks cannot be wished for as they are provided in a karmic way. Needless to say, we can wish for profits, success or recognition. It is often said that we all created our realities through our thoughts and achieve it all in doing so, or that we may order "for free" in the universe using the right thoughts or rituals. While a large number of people have found help in such approach, many still remain disappointed. It has helped the people whose soul code already bubbled up and flowed upon wish, constantly developing and further evolving. Conversely, those whose soul code awaits liberation and their wishes to become reality, remain frustrated. Time plays no role for the unbridled soul. We can ignite the soul code almost immediately and bring it to full development. Being aware of it is what really matters. Then it operates without any constraints. Before we resource to wishing oracles as the fastest way to a heart's wish fulfillment, we should concern ourselves with the state of our soul. This is often faster than the constant demand and unsuccessful waiting.

Wishes can come true. We are creating their reality through the activation of soul codes. If you have internalized my remarks, if you, dear reader, manage at least to recognize the soul code, you can choose the path of wishes, treading the "order" in creation - whatever wish you may have.

ORDERS IN CREATION

The readers of my book know by now that it is not about the appropriate formulation of wishes. Wishes will always come true when they correlate to the soul evolution status or are suitable for development of the soul code. The real challenge does not lie not finding the appropriate wish formulation but in adopting a constructive approach to its fulfillment. First of all, the soul code should be as active as possible, so that wish fulfillment is a matter of course. It is probably set in motion or accelerated among those who read this book and understand its messages. Completing the exercises described can further develop it.

To conclude my remarks, I would like to offer shorthand for wish formulation, which corresponds to the soul code. If you have a heart's desire and believe in the soul code, keep it in mind and foster it every day, as you will also experience the fulfillment of desire. Consider first the formulation of your wish. The words you choose are irrelevant. If you understand your own wish, the instance that receives it will do so as well. If your soul code is already bubbling and flowing, it is sufficient to have one wish. It will come true by itself. The following steps may prove helpful to active a sleeping soul code.

Six steps of wishing

1. **Express your wish!**

   First of all, try to find a quiet place for you to rest. You may make a brief meditation, if that helps to achieve your internal balance. Then, express you wish.

2. **Activation of the soul code of love!**

   Think of a person who has done you wrong. Internally, wish him all the best in his life. Imagine he would fulfill the same desire or one that is specially relevant to him. Grant him the fulfillment of his wishes!

3. **Activation of the soul code of community!**

   Imagine you meet a large number of people who fulfilled the same wish. Visualize yourself feeling comfortable with a group of like-minded, equally-recipient people. Congratulate all of them upon fulfilling the same wish.

4. *Activation of the soul code of resonance!*

   *Imagine how you use your fulfilled wishes
   to further explore your own live and foster
   the spiritual development. Create a picture
   of how, that which you have desired, besides the earthly comforts that may be connected to thereto, will represent an advance for your soul.*

5. *Activation of the soul code of karma!*

   *Imagine that creation sends you a package
   other than the one you ordered. Rest assured that the alternative wish fulfillment
   will be better than the formulated wish.
   Congratulate yourself in the creation for
   the best way and the best content of wish
   fulfillment.*

6. *Completion of the wish request!*

   *Promise yourself that you will remain on
   your path of soul development and spiritual evolution - even so when the fulfillment of your wish could lead to sluggish-
   ness.*

SUMMARY AND FINAL WORD

My remarks in the book intend to evidence that human existence is neither a product of chance nor a freak of nature but part of an overall plan of creation. The way we refer to the Creator or the highest instance of creation is mainly related to our own cultural and religious roots or upbringing. In my view, it is utterly irrelevant whether we advocate for one religion or another. I deem it of the utmost importance to draw a new picture of creation, where we humans are not its product but its executor. The creation is fulfilled through us. This is our original and only purpose, to serve the purpose of creation: the encounter of the earthly with the spiritual world at the same stage of development. This may sound presumptuous, or from the perspective of traditional religions appear nearly impossible, but it is my deep belief that humanity will one day accomplish such task. At the same time, I sense more and more people taking their first steps on the path of understanding, of evolution, of liberation of the soul codes.

On the other hand, I also wanted to clarify that, while the simple pursuit of worldly success and wish-fulfillment is understandable and justified given human nature, it is not enough to develop one's own soul and to contribute to the community of souls. However, this is not a bad news after all. It also does not mean that the wishes for an event or a success would be harder than the wishing oracle or affirmations promise. However, it is important to understand that there are no rituals, formulations, or trainable behavior to make wishes come true. It is the state of our soul that decides what we can accomplish and understand. While we recognize the soul code and keep it in mind, we foster the development of our soul and thus the development of the community of souls on earth and in the spiritual world.

If I could convey with my remarks that this is only an alternative yet not harder path to the beaten one, I would have reached my goal. Those readers that recognize the presence of a simple soul code in them and that are also willing to accept and further develop it, will achieve personal happiness and success. You will experience internal liberation of external wish fulfillment, while making a significant contribution to the community of souls by the path of convergence of earthly existence with the spiritual world.

ABOUT THE AUTHOR

Taylor Moone is a trance medium and spiritual teacher. In his seminars in Switzerland and on lecture tours throughout Europe and the U.S., he captivates the audience with messages from the spiritual world, which he receives in meditation and séances. The basic message of this world states that every individual has the task of developing his own soul and thus the development of a higher level of cognitive ability. Life on earth is the path to our soul´s journey home to the spiritual world. Every single soul develops over many earthly lives and contributes to the higher development of the community of souls. Taylor Moone shares with thousands interested in his knowledge of the soul code, that it is possible to recognize this development and to actively use it to obtain good fortune, achieve success, wish fulfillment, and healing.

www.seelencode.com

© Verlag Ingo Simon, St. Wendel, www.verlagis.de
Paperback, ISBN 978-3-943323-02-3